# Bird Designs
# Stained Glass Pattern Book

## Carolyn Relei

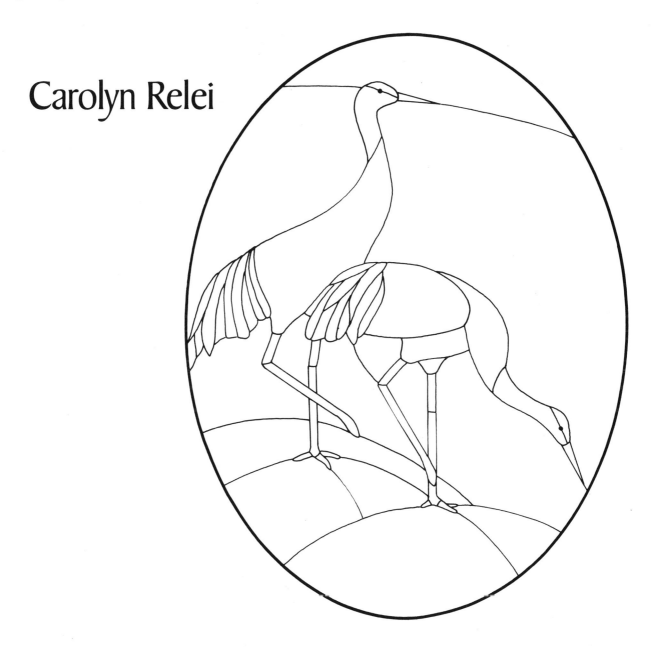

Dover Publications, Inc., New York

Copyright © 1989 by Dover Publications, Inc.
All rights reserved under Pan American and International Copyright Conventions.

Published in Canada by General Publishing Company, Ltd., 30 Lesmill Road, Don Mills, Toronto, Ontario.
Published in the United Kingdom by Constable and Company, Ltd.

*Bird Designs Stained Glass Pattern Book* is a new work, first published by Dover Publications, Inc., in 1989.

DOVER *Pictorial Archive* SERIES

Manufactured in the United States of America
Dover Publications, Inc., 31 East 2nd Street, Mineola, N.Y. 11501

Library of Congress Cataloging-in-Publication Data

Relei, Carolyn.
    Bird designs stained glass pattern book / Carolyn Relei.
        p.          cm.—(Dover pictorial archive series)
    ISBN 0-486-25947-1
    1. Glass craft.   2. Glass painting and staining—Patterns.
    3. Birds in art.   1. Title.   II. Series.
    TT298.R44   1989
    748.5—dc19                              88-26717
                                            CIP

# PUBLISHER'S NOTE

People have long been fascinated by the lightness, even airiness, of birds. This quality finds an unusually apt resonance in the bright and atmospheric translucency of stained glass, which is also capable of suggesting quite effectively the rich and complex colorations and textures found on birds.

These designs by stained glass designer Carolyn Relei convincingly outline the essential character of each bird. To determine the colorations to be used you should consult paintings and photographs of birds, or else just let your imagination soar! The front cover shows one of the mallard designs handled with naturalistic colors.

This collection of 77 newly created designs, in an array of different shapes, is well suited to a number of crafts applications including mobiles, ornaments, lightcatchers, windows, mirrors, candle shelters, panels, lampshades and fanlights. The book is intended as a supplement to stained glass instruction books (such as *Stained Glass Craft* by J. A. F. Divine and G. Blachford, Dover Publications, Inc., 0-486-22812-6). All materials needed, including general instructions and tools for beginners, can usually be purchased from local craft and hobby stores listed in your Yellow Pages.

Hummingbird with Roses

1

Indigo Bunting

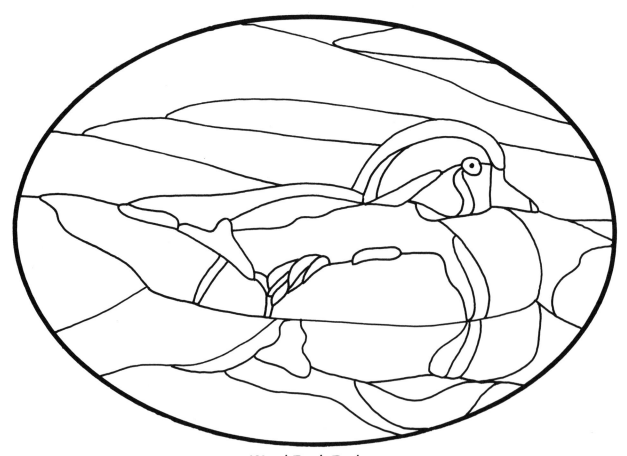

Wood Duck Drake

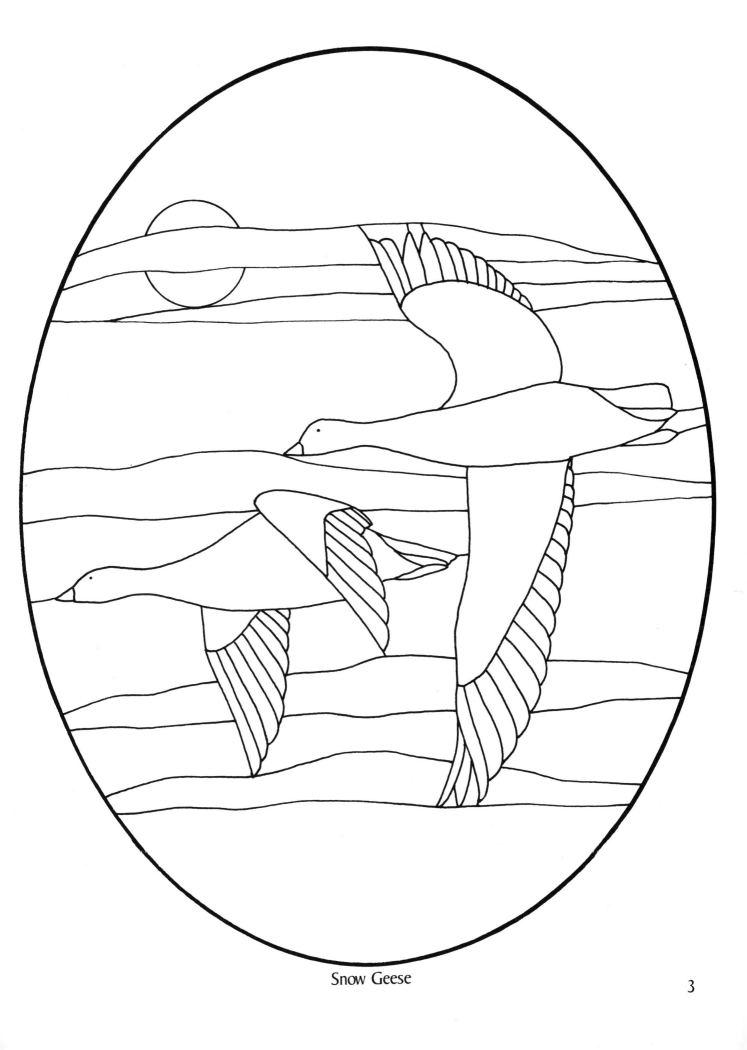

Snow Geese

3

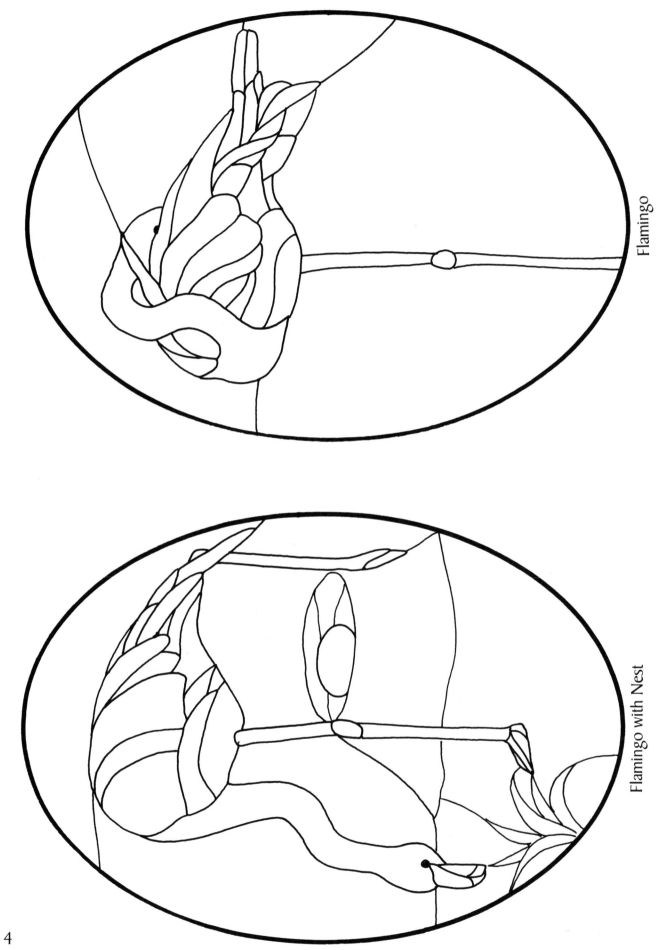

Flamingo

Flamingo with Nest

4

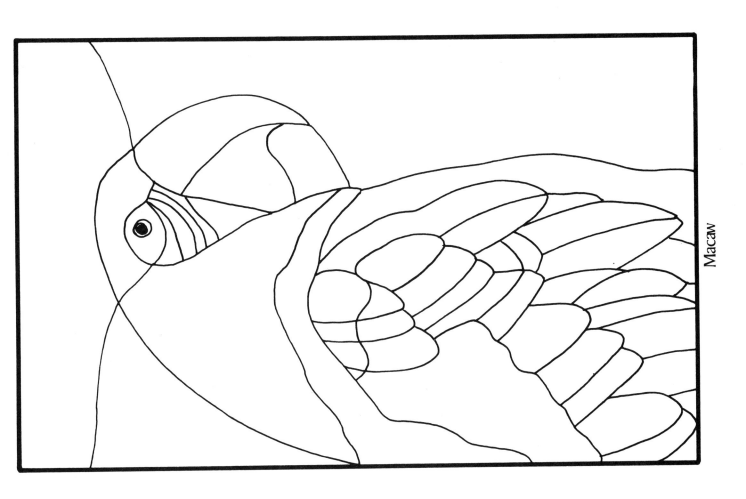

Macaw

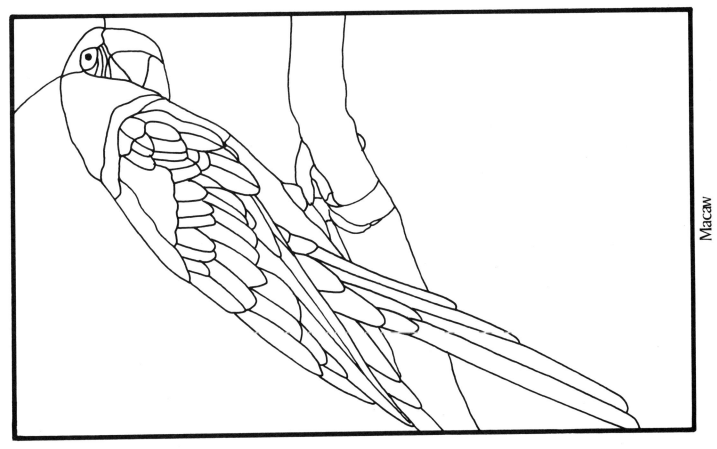

Macaw

5

Wood Ducks

Peacock

Scarlet Macaw

7

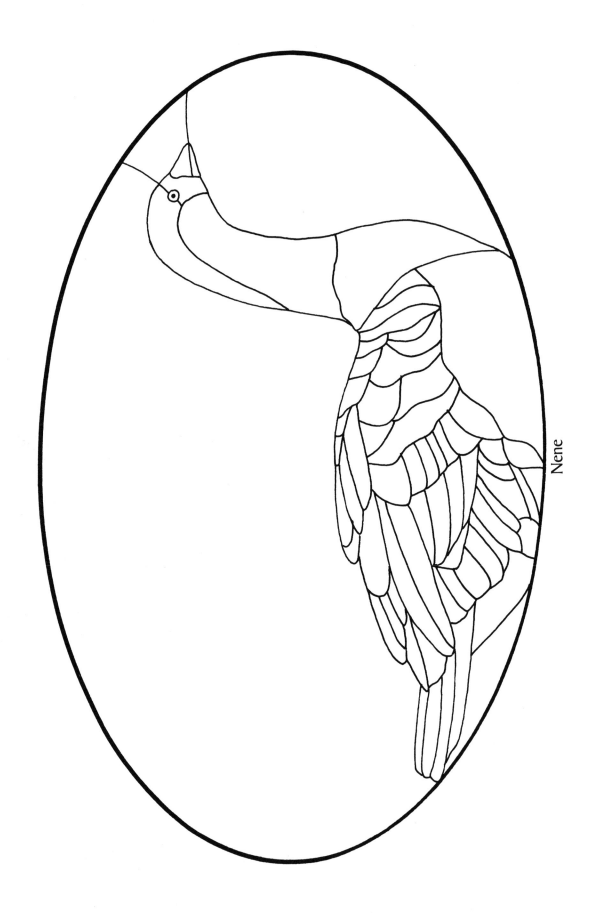

Nene

8

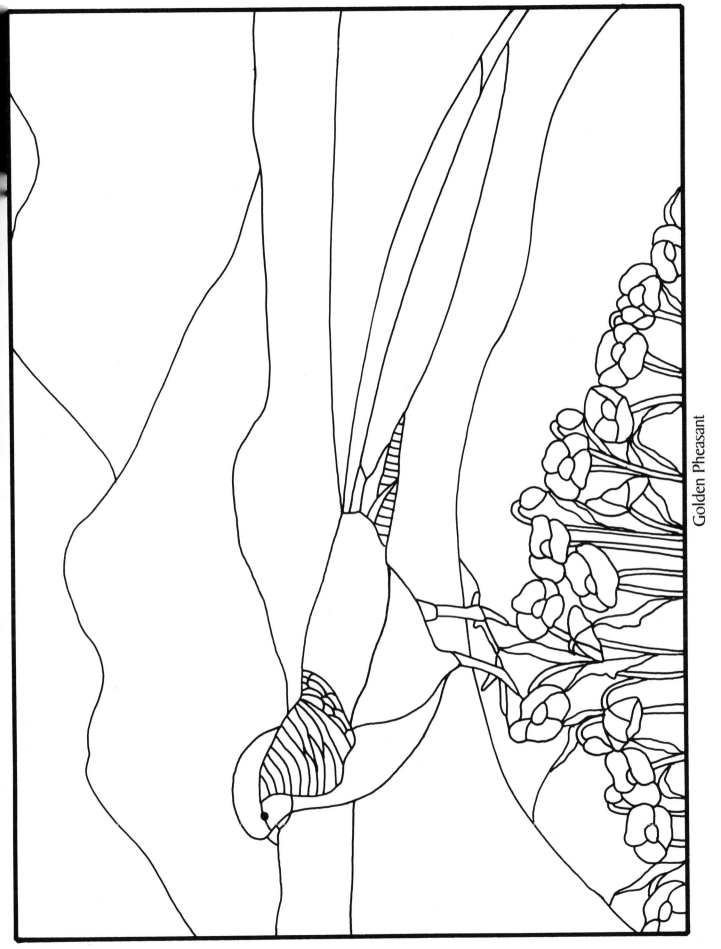

Golden Pheasant

9

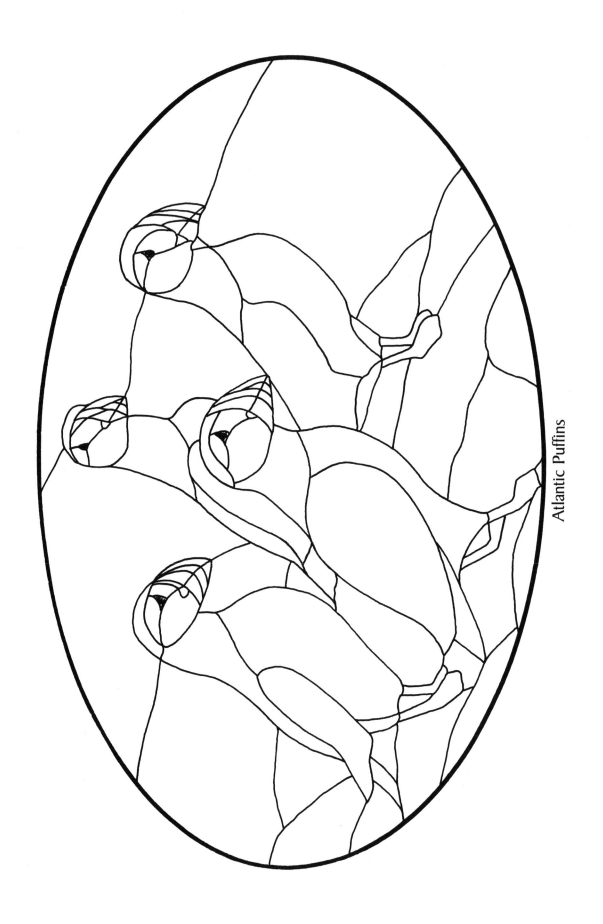

Atlantic Puffins

Mandarin Ducks

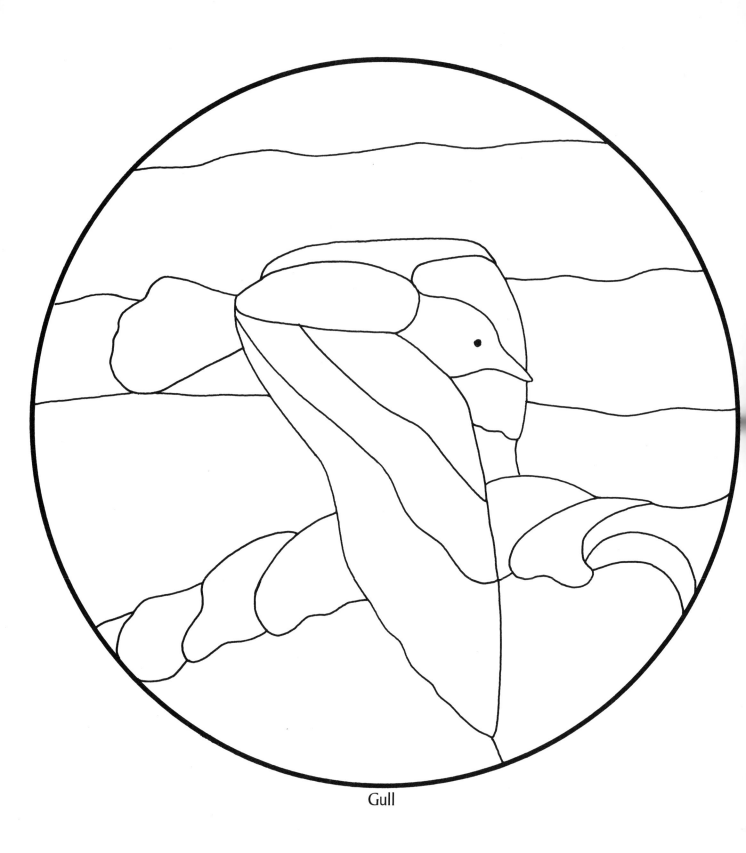

Gull

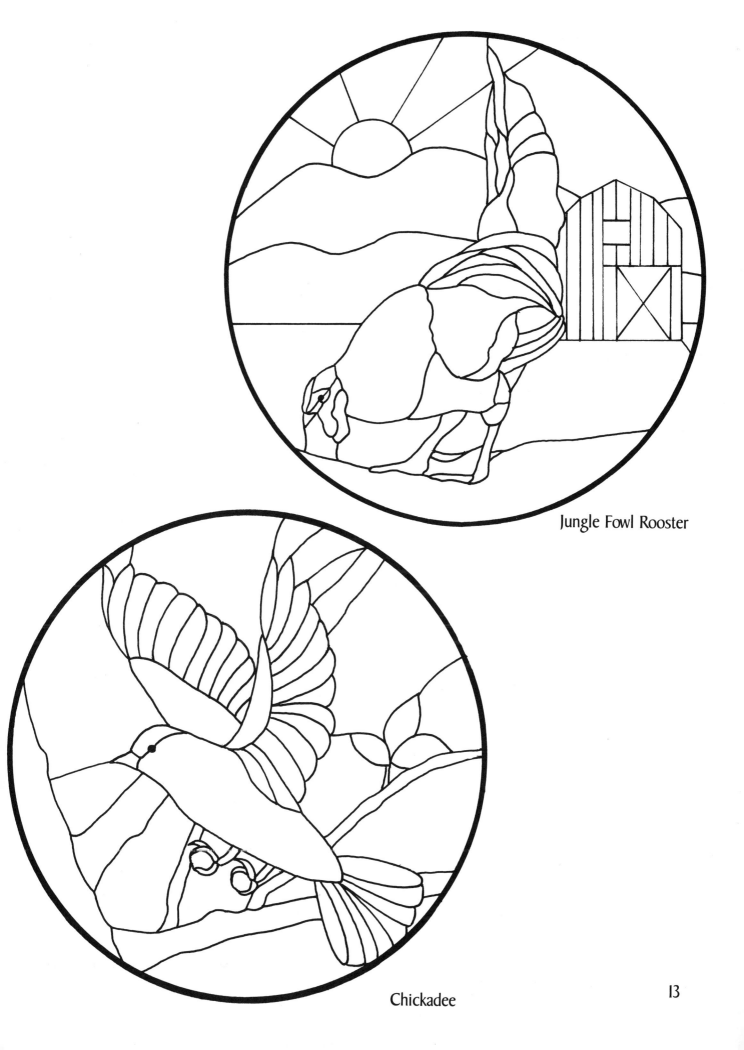

Jungle Fowl Rooster

Chickadee

13

Canada Geese

Jungle Fowl

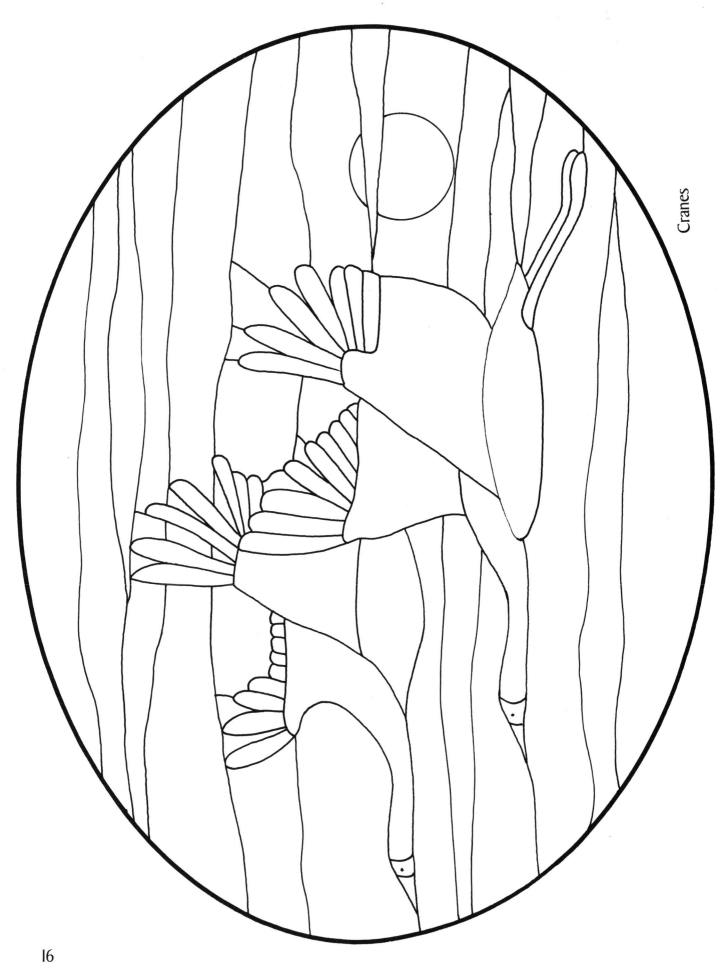

Cranes

Mute Swan with Cygnets

17

Canada Geese

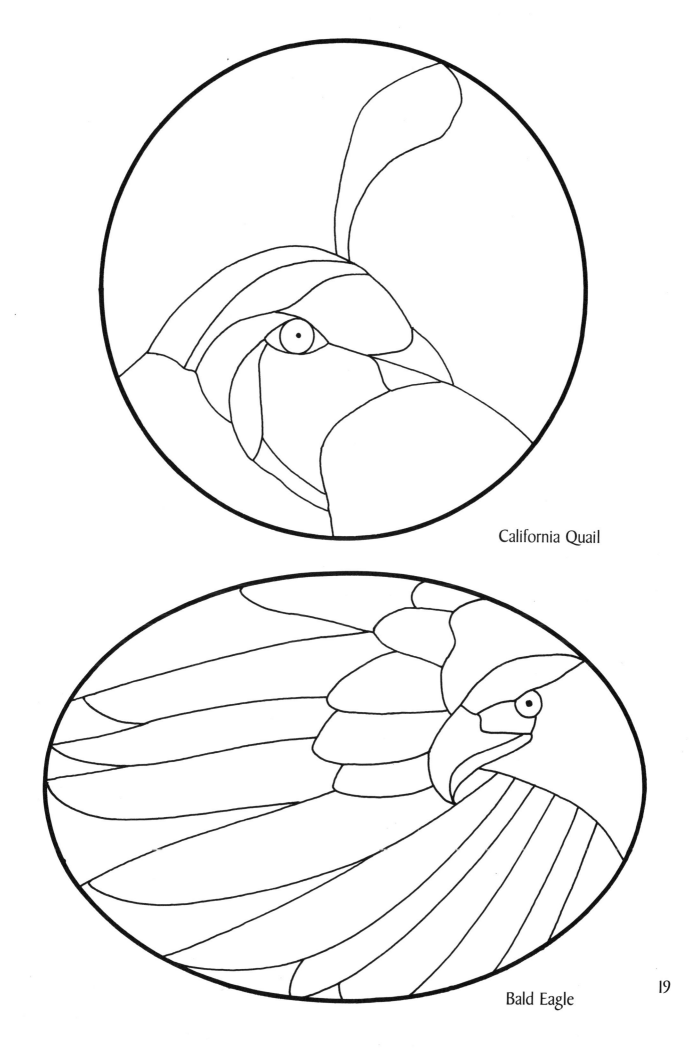

California Quail

Bald Eagle

19

Peahen

Mute Swan

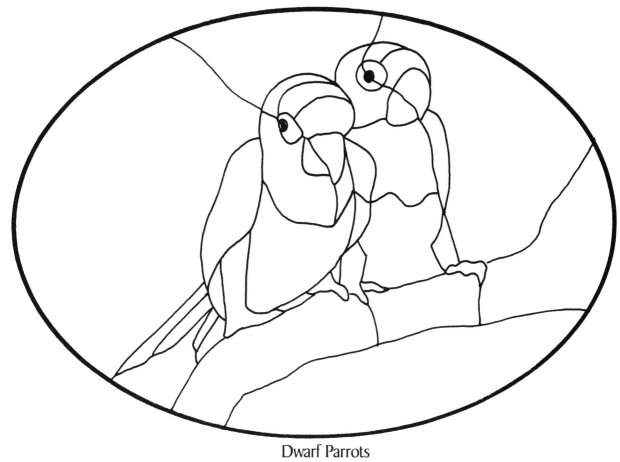

Dwarf Parrots

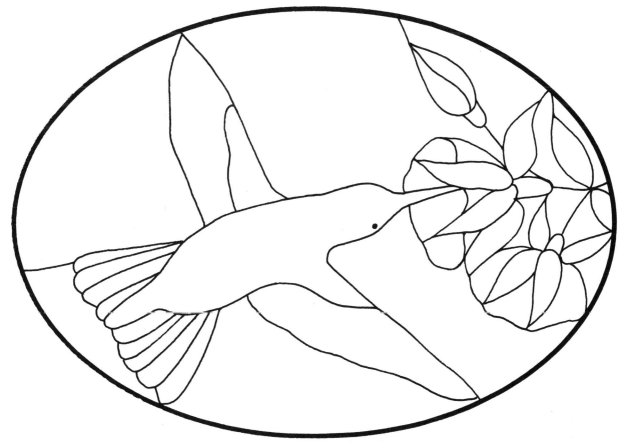

Hummingbird and Fuchsias

Adélie Penguins

California Brown Pelicans

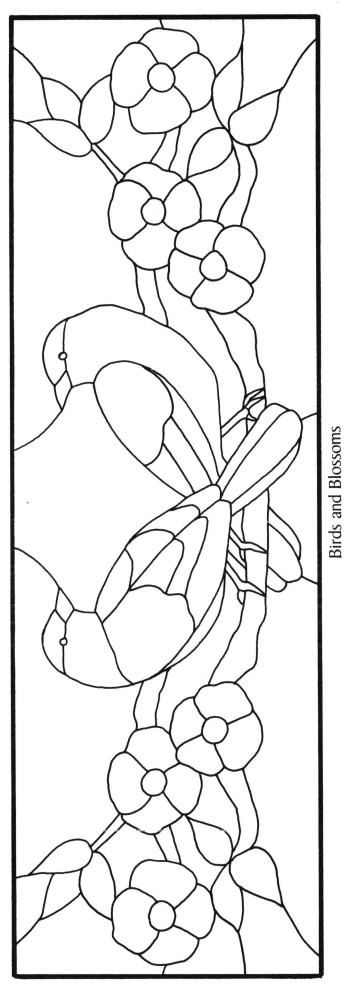

Birds and Blossoms

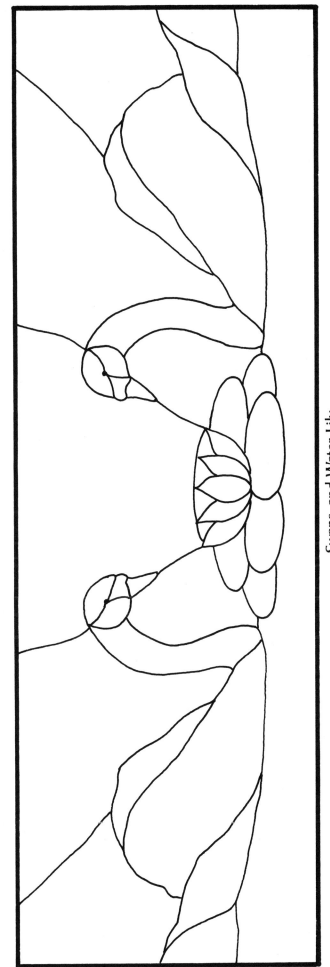

Swans and Water Lily

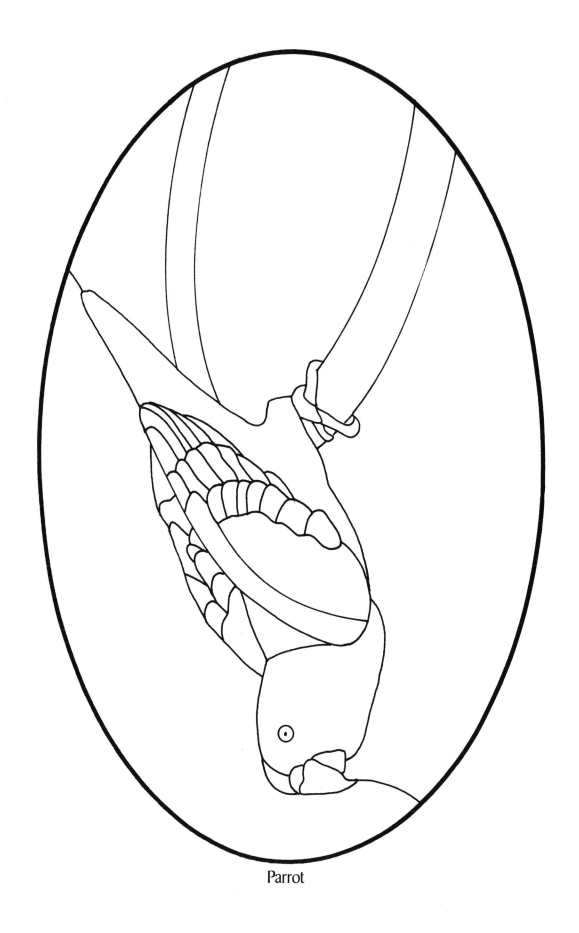

Parrot

Bird with Dogwood Blossoms

25

Mallards

Heron

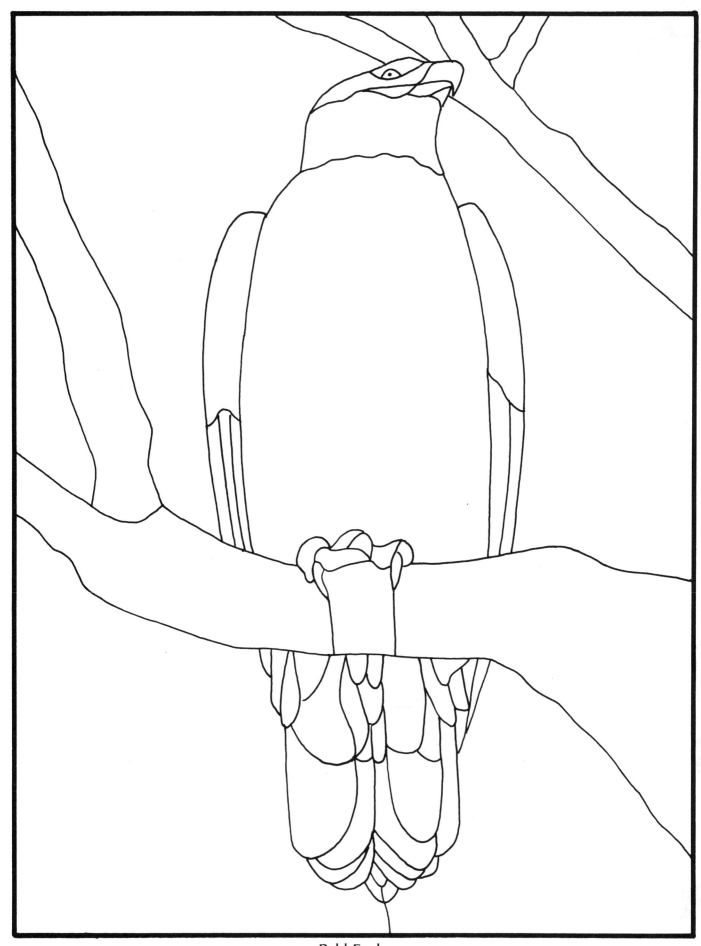

28               Bald Eagle

Mallard Hen

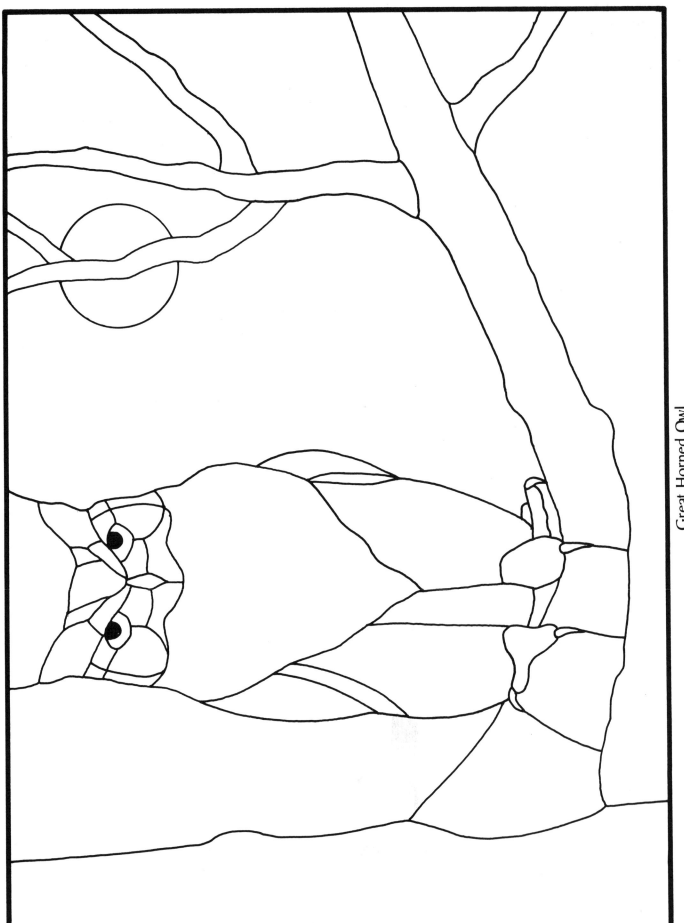

Great Horned Owl

Pintail Duck Drake

Plymouth Rock Rooster

Mallards

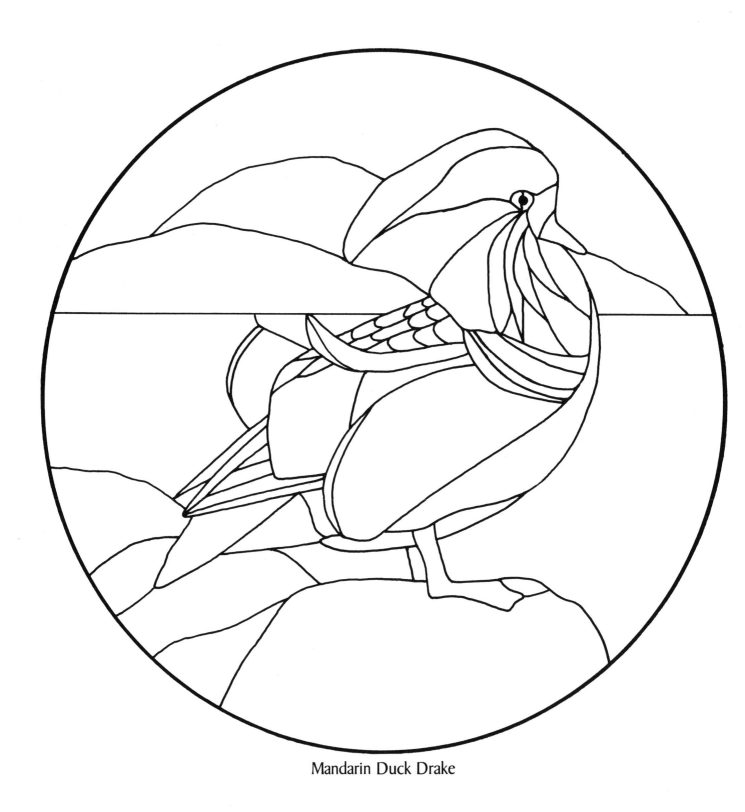

Mandarin Duck Drake

Dalmatian Pelican

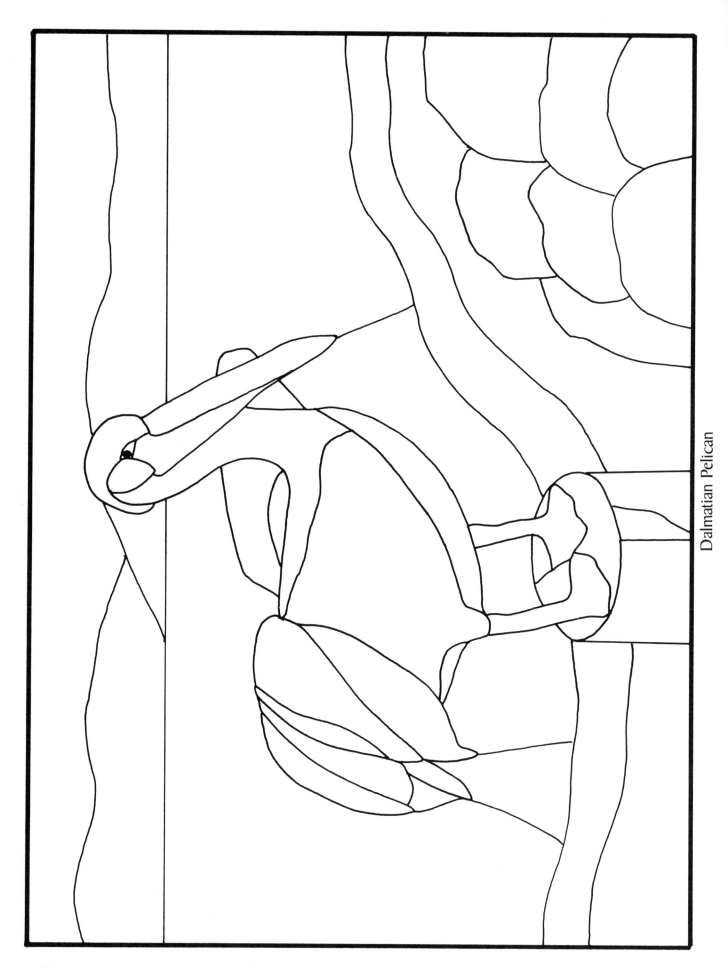

Dalmatian Pelican

36

Mallards

Mallards

Whistling Swans

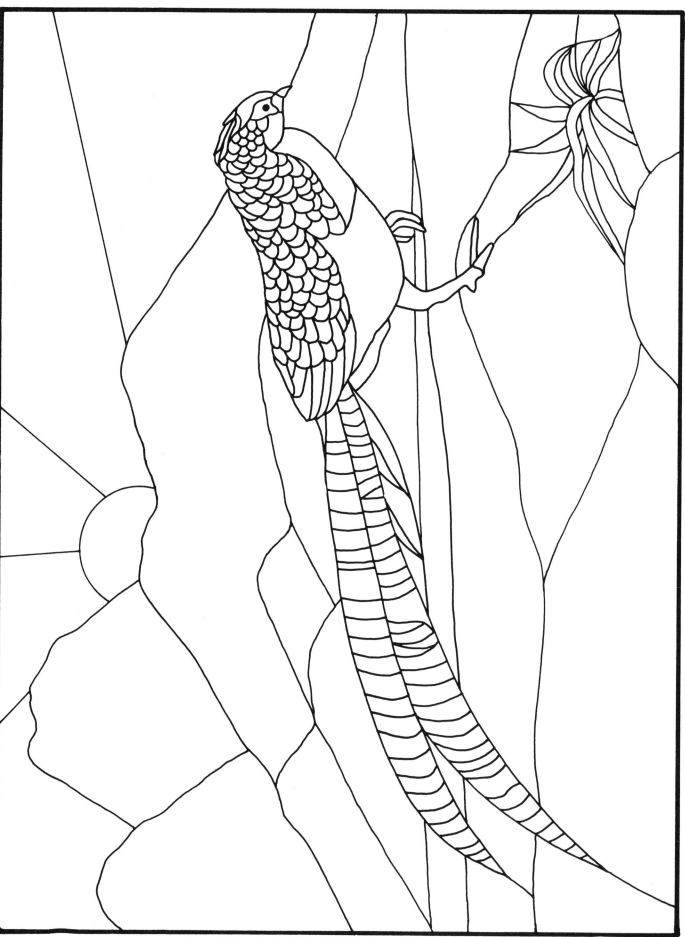

Lady Amherst Pheasant

Peacock Arch

Peacocks

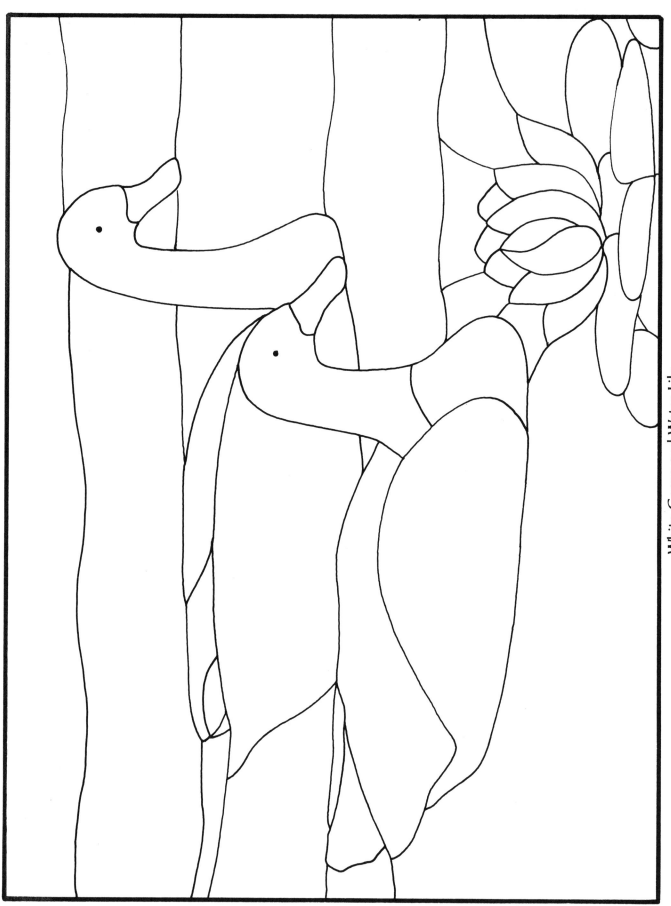

White Geese and Water Lily

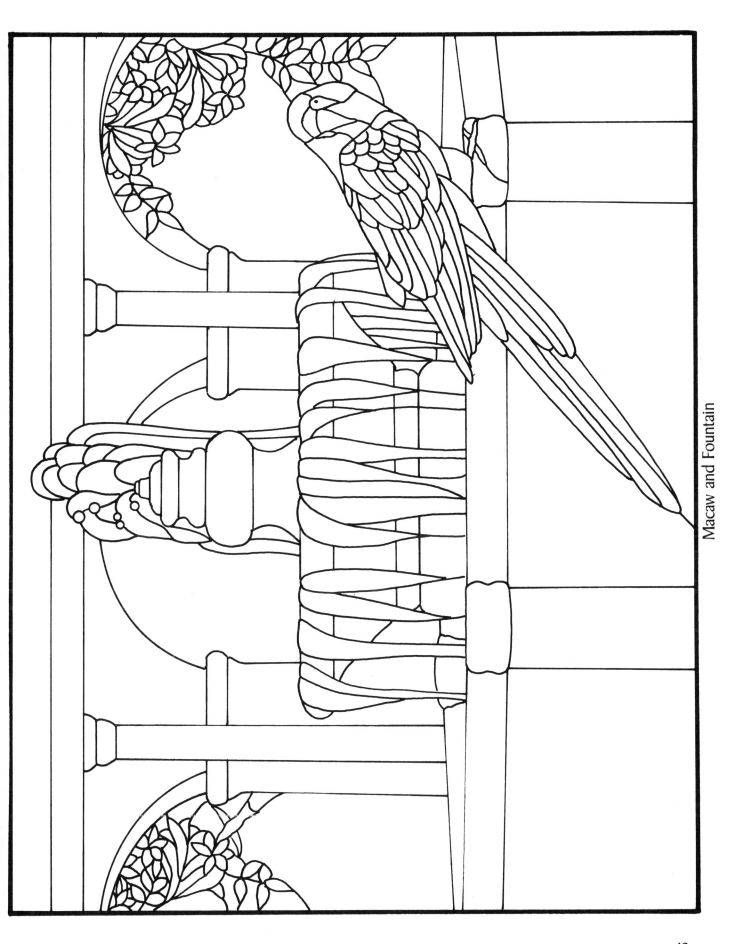

Macaw and Fountain

43

Hummingbirds with Morning Glories

Mallards

45

Snowy Egret

46

Ducks

Mandarin Duck Drake

Great Hornbills

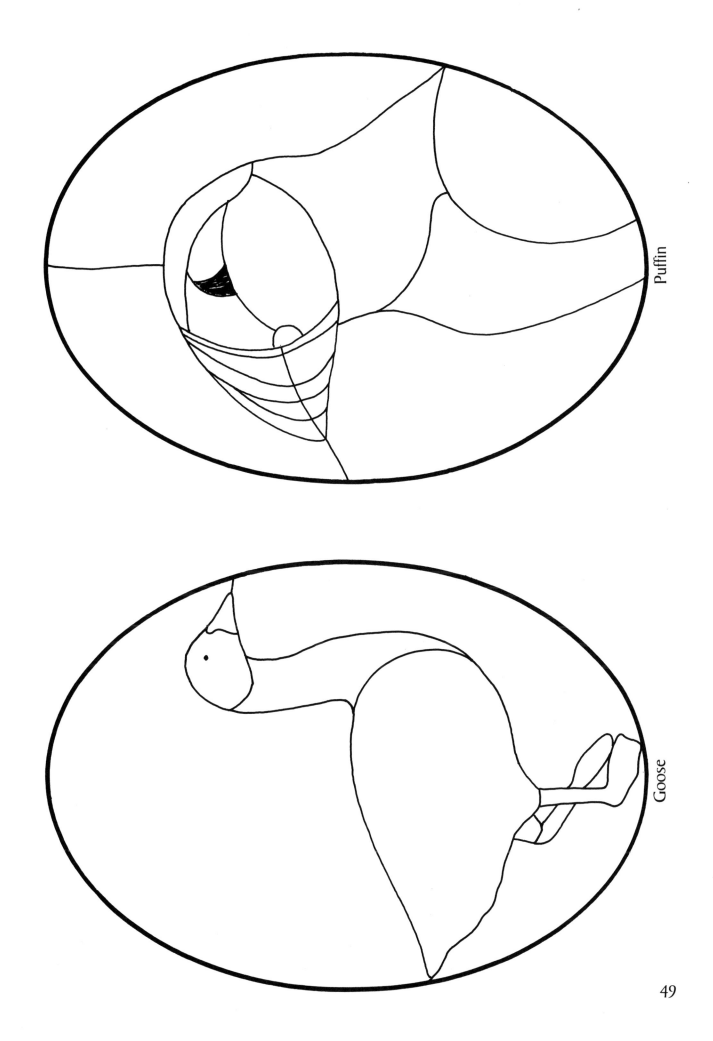

Puffin

Goose

49

50 Peacock and Blossoms

Cockatiel

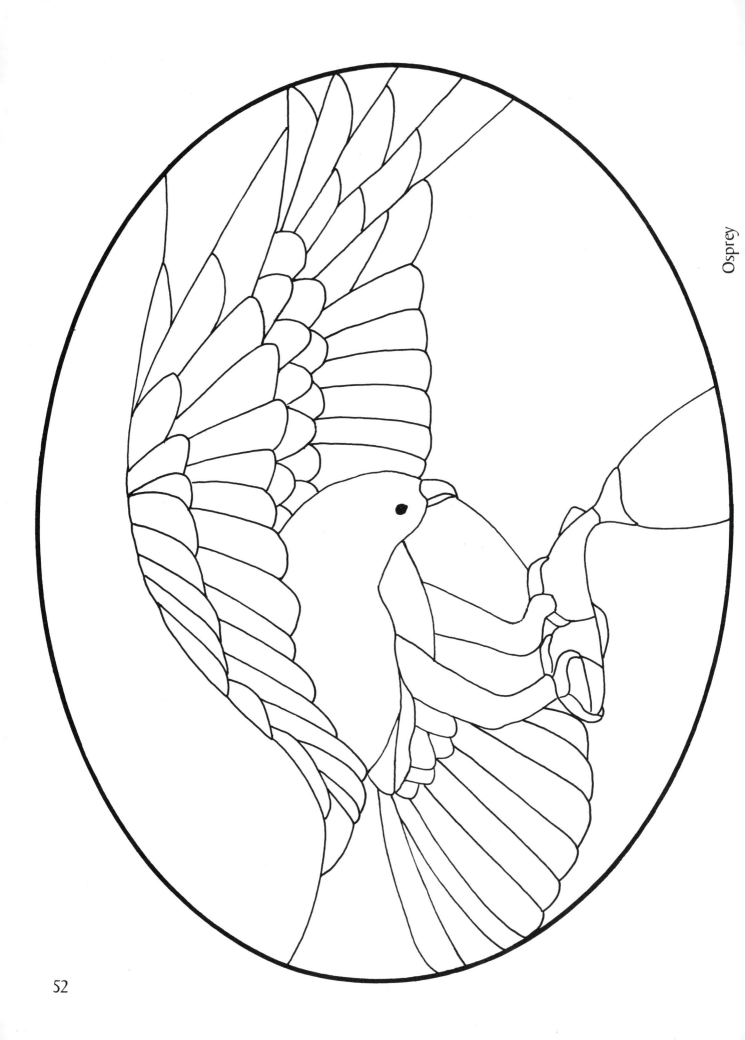

Osprey

52

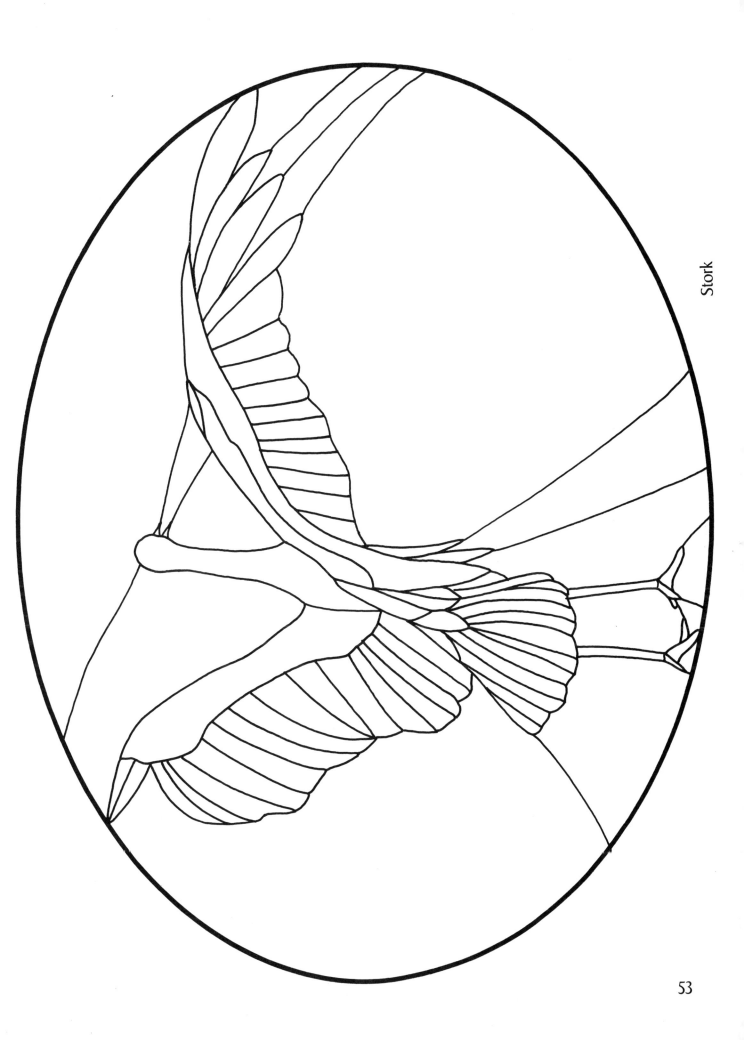

Stork

Ring-necked Pheasant

Canada Goose

55

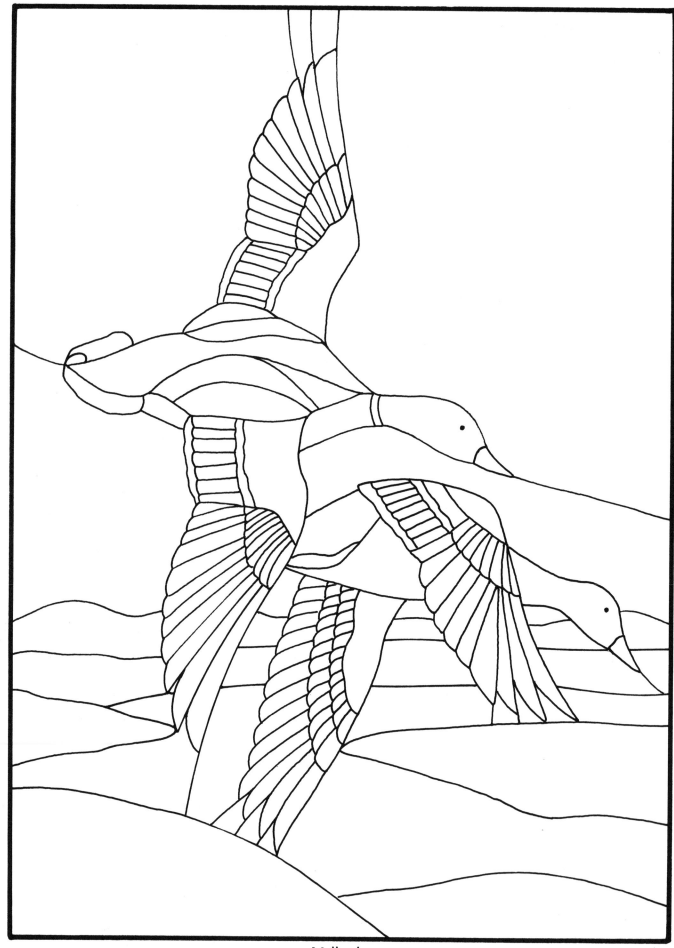

Mallards

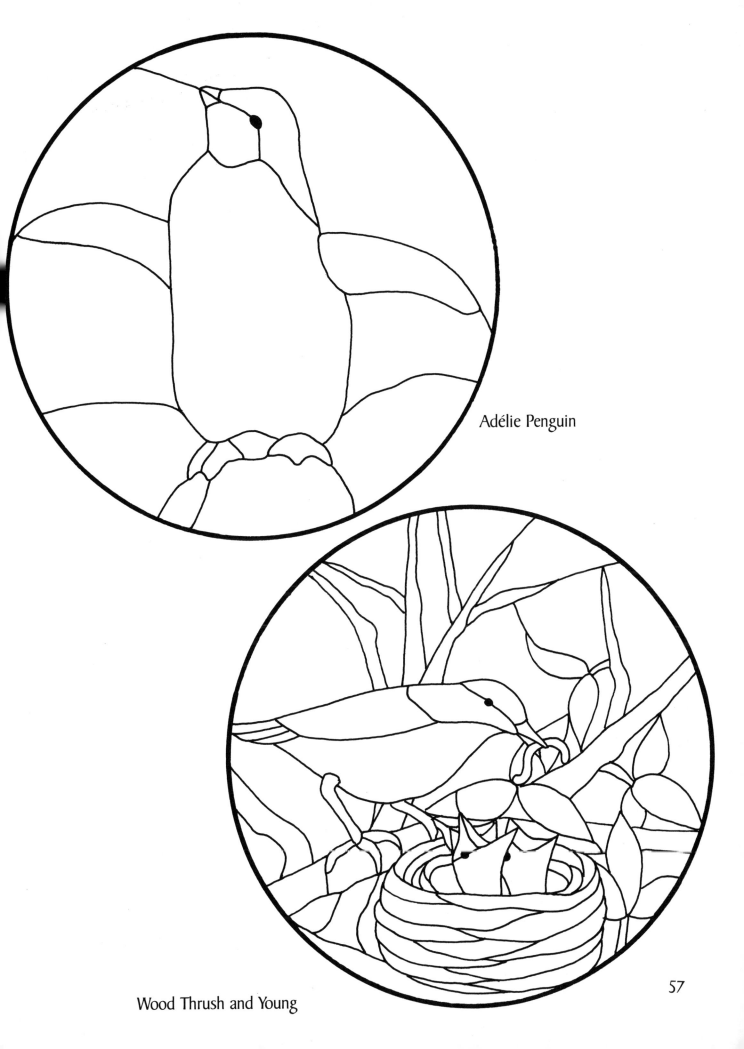

Adélie Penguin

Wood Thrush and Young

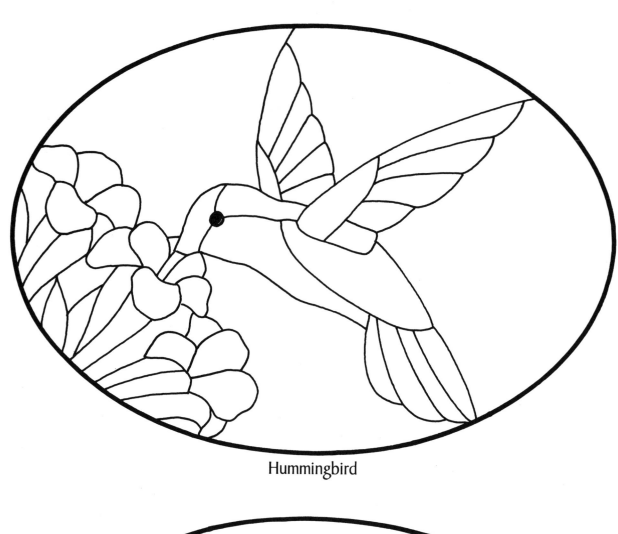

Hummingbird

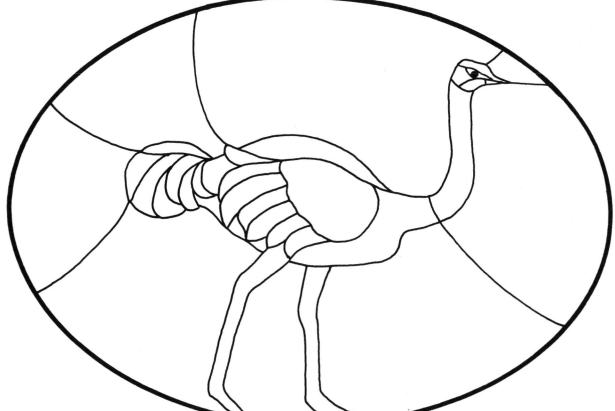

Ostrich

Toucan

59

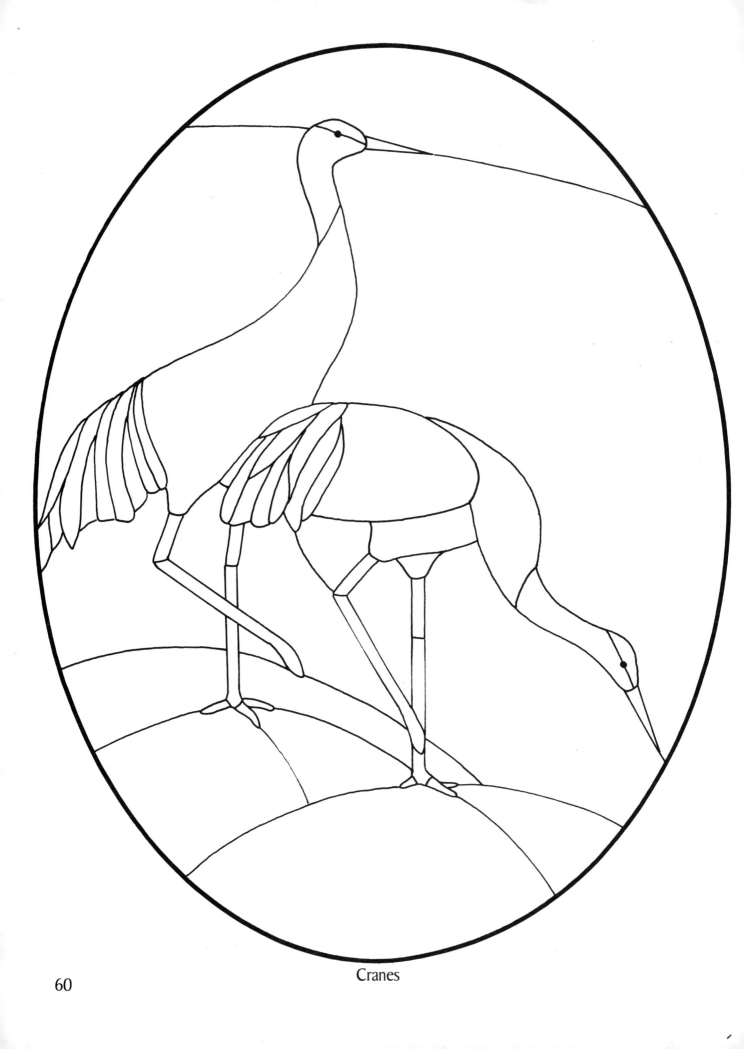

Cranes